NEBULAE

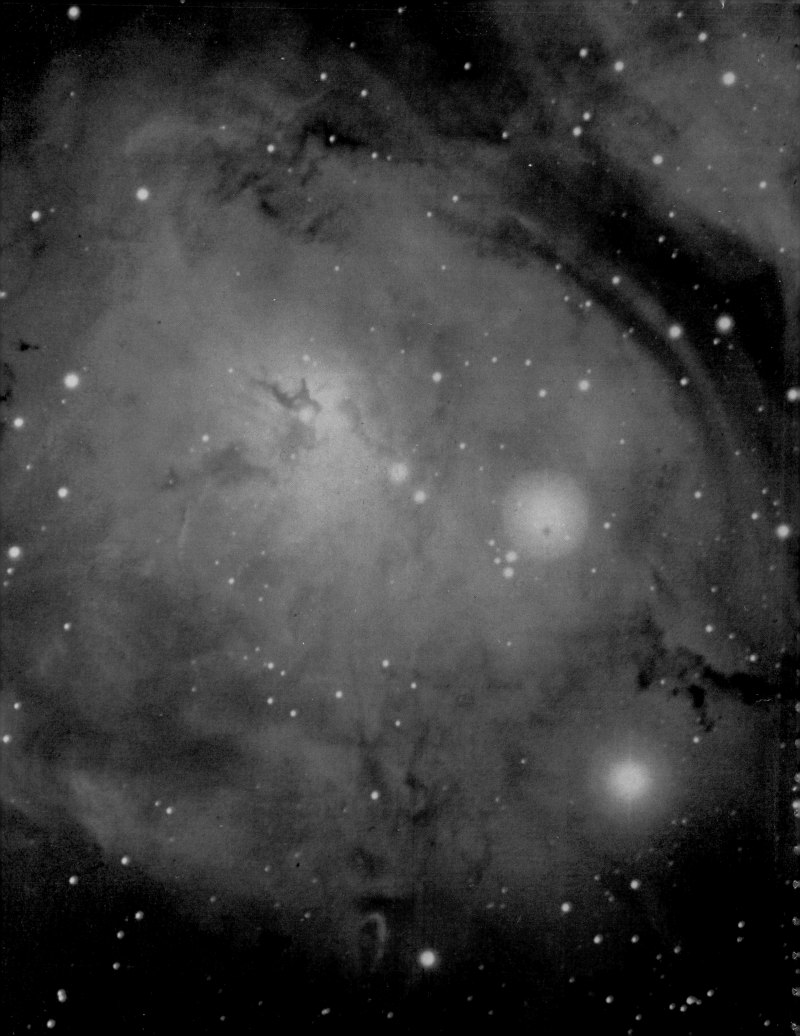

NECIA H. APFEL

NEBULAE

THE BIRTH & DEATH OF STARS

LOTHROP, LEE & SHEPARD BOOKS   NEW YORK

TITLE PAGE PHOTOGRAPH: **The Lagoon Nebula, located in the constellation Sagittarius. It is known for the dark channel dividing the brighter area.**

ACKNOWLEDGMENTS Photograph on page 29 courtesy of the Adler Planetarium of Chicago; pages 2–3, 11, 12, 15, 19, 20, 21, 22, 25, 26, 31, 32, 33, 38, 42, and 47 © California Institute of Technology; page 28 courtesy of EARTH SCENES/Anthony Bannister; page 16 courtesy of the Lick Observatory; pages 41 and 45 courtesy of NASA; pages 27, 35, 37, and 44 courtesy of the National Optical Astronomy Observatories; page 8 courtesy of Robert Provin; page 6 courtesy of Steven Wissler; page 9 courtesy of Yosemite Collections, National Park Service.

First Edition

1 2 3 4 5 6 7 8 9 10

Library of Congress Cataloging in Publication Data
Apfel, Necia H.   Nebulae: the birth and death of stars.
Bibliography: p.   Includes index. Summary: Describes how nebulae or clouds of dust particles and gases in space form from the residue of dying stars and how some nebulae contain matter from which stars are born.
1. Nebulae—Juvenile literature. [1. Nebulae.   2. Stars]   I. Title.
QB855.22.A64 1988   523.1'135   86-33765
ISBN 0-688-07228-3   ISBN 0-688-07229-1 (lib. bdg.)

TO MY GRANDSON BENJAMIN

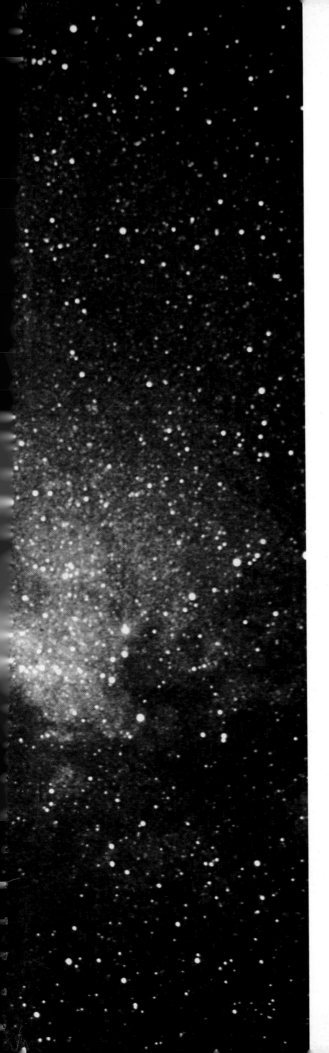

Look up at the stars shining brightly in the clear night sky. They all appear to be so close together. With your out-stretched hand you can cover perhaps ten or twenty of them. But the stars are really very far apart. They look so near to one another only because they are so far away from us. Actually, billions and billions of miles separate the stars. And it is here in the spaces between the stars, where the sky appears black and empty, that our story begins.

A small section of the Milky Way. Each tiny dot of light is a star. Some are many times bigger than our sun, which is also a star.

The Beehive Cluster, a large, bright group of about two hundred stars in the
constellation Cancer.

Those dark regions of the sky are not as empty as they look. Tiny particles of matter, as fine as dust, float around in these spaces. These particles of matter are so small you couldn't see them even if they were right in front of your eyes. Scientists must use very powerful microscopes to see particles that are as small as the kind found between the stars.

8

Not only are these specks of matter very tiny, they are usually very thinly spread out. A volume of space the size of a small marble may contain only a few dozen particles. The rest of the space in each such marble-size region is empty. By comparison, each marble-size volume of air that we breathe contains more than a billion billion particles. However, because the space between the stars is so enormous compared to the space occupied by the air around the earth, the total number of particles out there is far greater than the number of particles in our air.

Moonrise over a valley. The air near the earth's surface has the greatest number of particles.

If these tiny bits of matter always stayed so thinly scattered, our story would be over. But sometimes they are pushed closer together. This can happen when a star explodes. The force of the explosion sends strong shock waves out into space. These shock waves push the tiny particles between the stars closer together. In each marble-size volume of space that formerly contained only about two dozen particles, there might now be a few thousand particles. Once these particles are pushed together, they tend to stay together. And when the concentration of particles in a large volume of space increases this much, a cloud forms. Some of these clouds of particles can be seen from earth.

The Omega Nebula in the constellation Sagittarius is one of the clouds of particles that lies between the stars. Because of its shape, it is sometimes called the Swan Nebula.

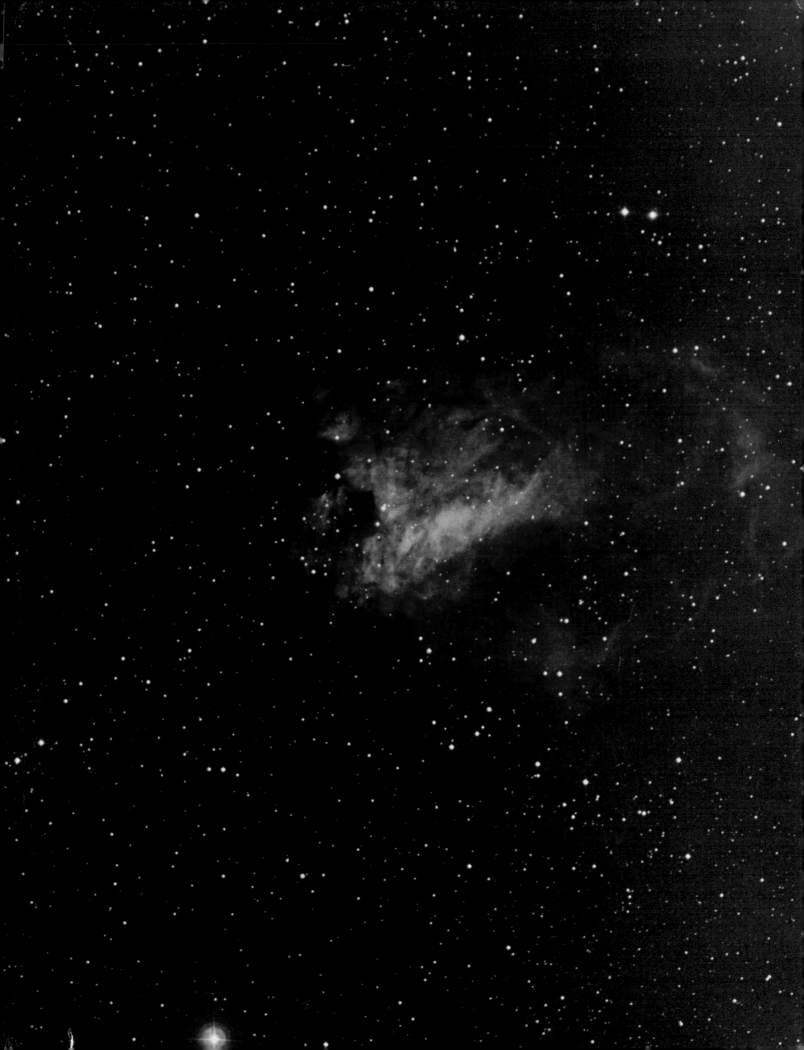

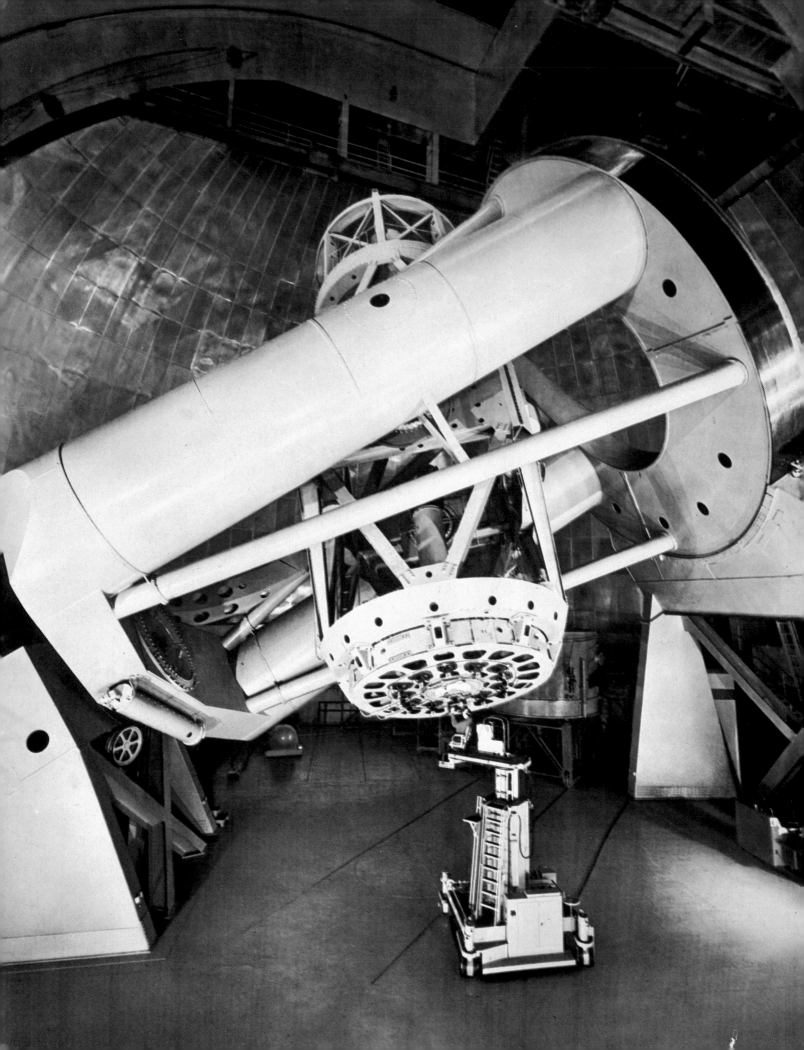

A cloud of particles between the stars is called a nebula. *Nebula* is the Latin word for "cloud." Two or more such clouds are called nebulae. You can see a few of these nebulae, like the Orion Nebula, with a small telescope or with your naked eye. But to reveal the true beauty of these clouds in space, you need a camera attached to a large telescope. All of the photographs of nebulae that you see in this book were taken with such equipment; the photographic film was exposed for many minutes or even hours.

The two-hundred-inch Hale telescope on Mount Palomar in California. Note the astronomer sitting in the elevating chair.

The particles of matter in a nebula, just like the more spread-out particles that float between the stars, are too tiny for us to see. But if there is a bright star within or near the nebula, it shines on the nebula particles and illuminates them. We still can't see any individual particles, but when billions of them are lit up by the star, the beautiful nebula is revealed. This is what is happening in the Orion Nebula, named after the constellation Orion in which it is found. It is one of the few nebulae that can be seen without a large telescope. With a good pair of binoculars or a small telescope, you can tell that the Orion Nebula is quite different in appearance from the stars around it.

The Orion Nebula is the best-known and most studied nebula in the sky.

We can see the Orion Nebula because embedded in it are four very bright stars that together are called the Trapezium. Although these four stars are difficult to see because they are deep within the nebula, their light is mainly responsible for letting us see the nebula. In addition, astronomers have detected more than three hundred less-bright stars within the Orion Nebula. All of these stars are very young. They probably started to form no more than about three hundred thousand years ago and may have begun shining only twenty thousand to twenty-five thousand years ago. These are very short time periods in astronomy, making this star cluster one of the youngest known.

The Trapezium star group in the central section of the Orion Nebula illuminates the nebula material.

Underneath the cloud layers in the Orion Nebula, hidden from our view, are several small, very dense clumps or globules of nebula material. Like the nebula itself, these globules are made of the same kind of dust and gas particles found scattered between the stars. But the particles in the globules are much closer together than the other particles in the Orion Nebula. These globules are believed to be proto-stars, the beginnings of stars that have not yet become big enough and hot enough to start shining. But they already have enough gravitational pull to draw in more and more particles from the rest of the nebula, thus growing larger and larger. In time, these globules will become real stars and will radiate light as the Trapezium stars do.

New stars may one day form in the Star Queen Nebula in the constellation Serpens. Can you see the thronelike pinnacle near its center?

The Rosette Nebula in the constellation Monoceros.

Each of the dark globules embedded in the Rosette Nebula is already much larger than our solar system. But each globule will slowly grow smaller and more compact and dense as its gravitational force pulls the dust and gas particles inward toward its center. Someday, each globule may become a star or may even form a solar system something like our own.

20

Like the Orion Nebula, other nebulae are also "stellar nurseries," places where stars are forming. Globules of nebula material, much like those in the Orion Nebula, have been detected in the cloud layers of these nurseries. One famous stellar nursery is the Rosette Nebula in the constellation Monoceros. As in the Orion Nebula, a bright group of stars in its center illuminates the surrounding nebula particles.

The **Trifid Nebula** in the constellation Sagittarius is the kind of nebula in which globules may form. It is named for the dark rifts dividing the brighter starlit regions into three sections.

Sometimes a stellar nursery doesn't have any stars within it to light up the particles. Instead, because the nebula is so huge and because it has so many billions of particles, it blocks our view of the stars behind it, preventing us from seeing their light. This is similar to the way fog here on earth can prevent us from seeing objects that are far away.

The North American Nebula in the constellation Cygnus. Some of the starlight illuminating the nebula is blocked, giving it this familiar shape.

23

The Horsehead Nebula is an example of this kind of "dark" nebula. Its particles are no closer to each other than the particles in any other nebula. And they are the same kinds of particles found in other nebulae. But because there are no stars to light up the material in the Horsehead, it looks very dark. The light from stars behind the cloud outlines the nebula and allows us to see its unusual shape.

The Horsehead Nebula in the constellation Orion is the best-known example of a "dark" nebula.

Once stars start shining within a nebula, their radiation begins to push away the rest of the scattered particles in the nebula. That is why the Rosette Nebula resembles a roselike ring. The nebula material that is very close to the young stars will be pulled into them by their gravity. The rest of the matter will be blown away by the new stars' radiation. Then the stars will be able to shine clearly. But young stars like those in the Pleiades cluster have not yet rid themselves of this nebulosity, and it can be seen still clinging to them.

The Pleiades star cluster in the constellation Taurus.

The Tarantula Nebula in the Large Magellanic Cloud, a small galaxy near our own Milky Way Galaxy. This nebula is thirty times bigger than the Orion Nebula and may be a place where stars are forming.

We have learned that nebulae can be the beginning, the places where stars start to form. But a nebula can also form during the final part of a star's life. This occurs billions of years after the star is born. By then it has used up most of its fuel and can no longer continue to shine with a constant brilliance. It becomes unstable. Its light begins to vary in strength. The star expands and contracts and goes through all kinds of other changes. Several times during this process, the star may throw off a portion of its hot, glowing gases into space, but this cannot stabilize the star's ever-changing conditions.

27

Our sun, the closest star to us, will not change for billions of years.

Right now our sun shines with a nearly constant amount of energy, emitting the heat and light we need to live. But in about six billion years our sun will begin to change. It will have used up most of its energy-producing fuel and will start to become unstable. Then, like other small- and medium-size stars that are reaching the end of their lives and are becoming unstable, our sun will start spewing some of its hot gases into space.

28

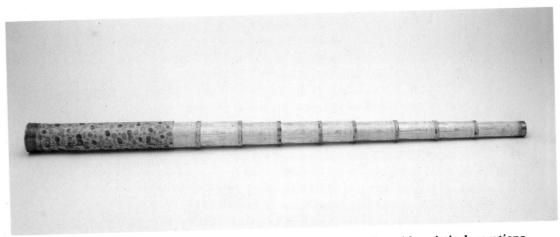

The earliest telescopes were hand-crafted. This small example, with artistic decorations on its tube, was made in Europe several hundred years ago.

If you could look through a large telescope at a small, unstable, aging star, it would appear to have a ring around it. The ring is the hot gases being shed by the star. But through many early telescopes these rings could not be detected so clearly. Instead, viewed through those crude telescopes, dying stars resembled planets. The stars appeared as small circles of light rather than tiny bright points. For this reason, they were called planetary nebulae. Although the name has never been changed, we now know that planetary nebulae have absolutely nothing to do with planets.

29

The most famous planetary nebula is the Ring Nebula in the constellation Lyra. It has a faint, small star in the center of a large ring. The star is slowly becoming even smaller as its ring gets larger. The star will eventually die out and stop shining, although this will take a very long time.

The Ring Nebula in the constellation Lyra.

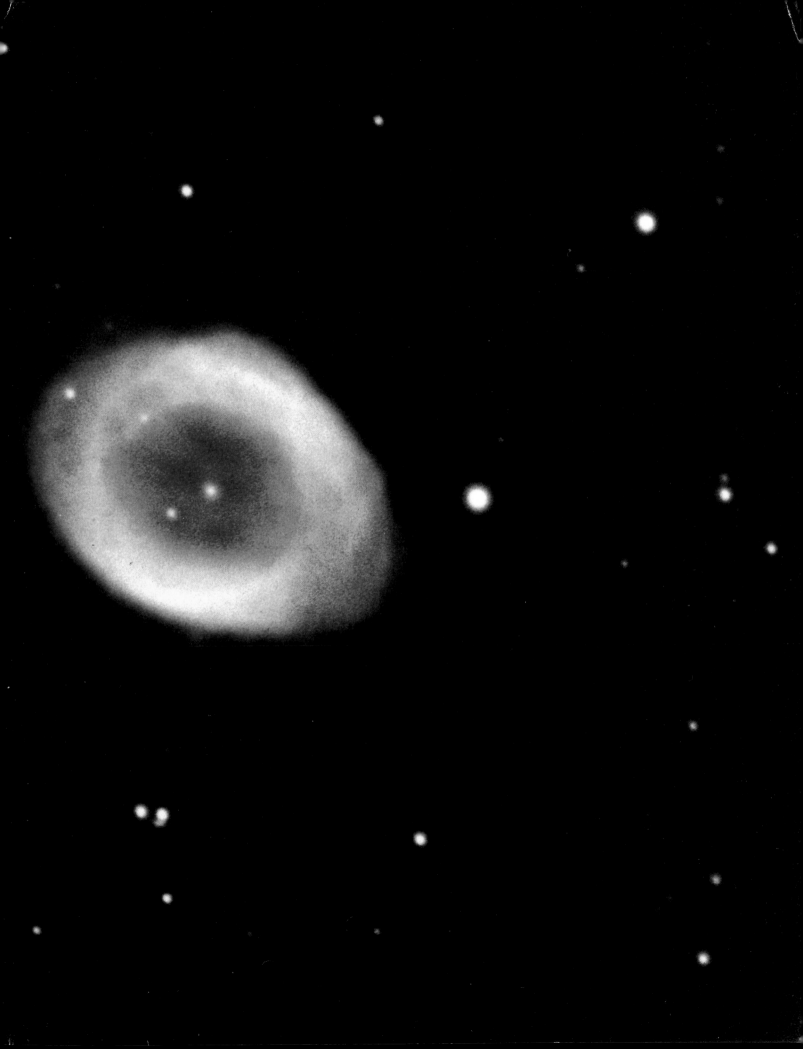

The ring of hot gases around a planetary nebula keeps expanding until the particles it is made of cool off. Then the ring stops glowing and the particles mingle with other scattered bits of matter that are already floating between the stars.

The Dumbbell Nebula in the constellation Vulpecula is one of the largest known planetary nebulae.

The Helical Nebula in the constellation Aquarius, another very large planetary nebula. It is sometimes called the Owl Nebula because of its appearance.

The ring we see around the Ring Nebula is about thirty times bigger than the distance between the earth and sun. It has been expanding outward from the star for about twenty thousand years. As with other planetary nebulae, the central star may have had rings around it before the present one developed, and it may produce more rings in the future.

The more massive stars, those that are many times larger than our sun, end their lives quite differently than do the smaller stars. When a big star runs out of energy and becomes unstable, it doesn't just quietly send rings of matter into space. Its end is extremely violent: It explodes. Instead of sending wave after wave of material out into the galaxy, the star blows up with one enormous BANG. The tremendous explosion causes shock waves that travel throughout the galaxy. These are the shock waves that push the tiny particles between the stars closer together to form new nebulae. The shock waves may not have any effect on other galaxies, but the explosion produces an extremely brilliant light that may be seen by astronomers using powerful telescopes here on earth. These stellar explosions are called supernovae.

In February 1987, a supernova exploded near the Tarantula Nebula. The picture on page 27 shows the Tarantula Nebula before the supernova appeared.

After a supernova explosion, all that is left of what was once an enormous star is a relatively small central core. The rest of the star's hot outer layers of gases have been forcefully thrust out into space at extremely rapid velocities, possibly more than one thousand miles per second! These gases are still very hot and still glow. These glowing supernova remnants can be seen through large telescopes. Some of them continue to glow for thousands of years.

A computer-generated image of the supernova remnant from Tycho's Star, whose explosion was seen in 1572. The star was named after Tycho Brahe, a Danish astronomer, who studied it.

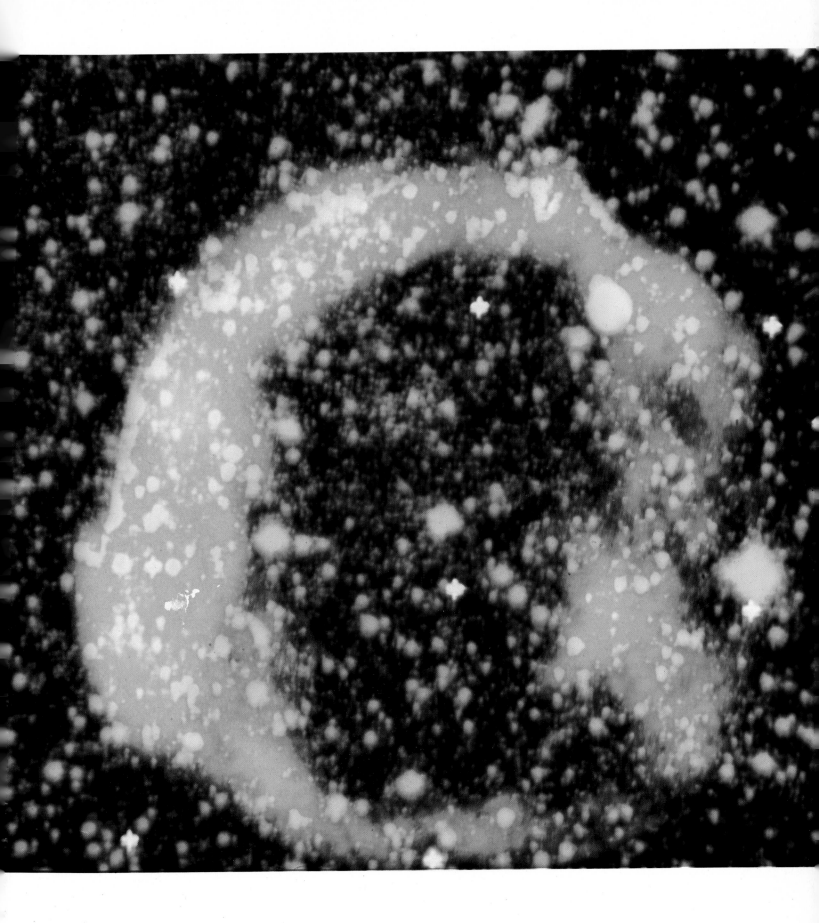

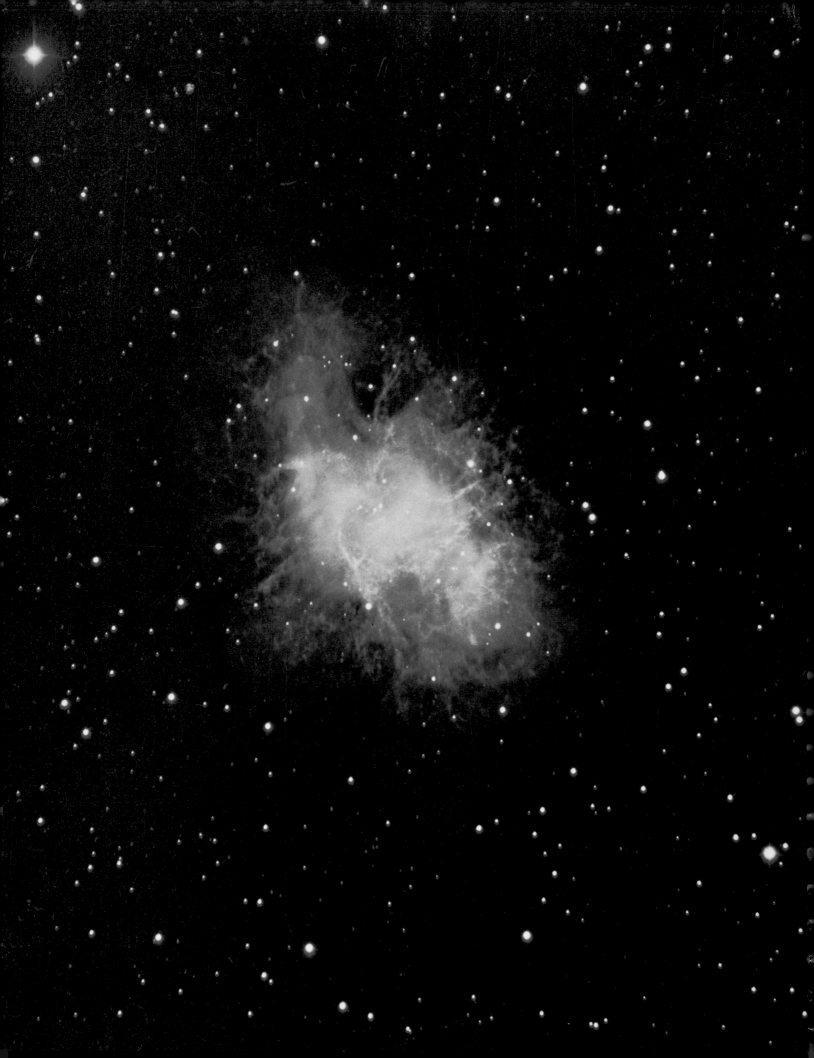

The most famous supernova remnant is the Crab Nebula. Records made by Chinese astronomers about a thousand years ago tell of seeing a brilliant new star in the constellation Taurus. Of course, it wasn't a new star that the astronomers saw, but one that had become thousands of times brighter when it exploded. Before its explosion it was invisible to the naked eye, and telescopes had not yet been invented. No wonder the astronomers thought it was a new star. The Latin word *nova* means "new."

The Crab Nebula in the constellation Taurus.

After several months the so-called new star gradually died away and could no longer be seen with the naked eye. But the Crab Nebula, a reminder of that violent explosion long ago, can still be seen through a telescope. Its gases are still very hot and it is these glowing gases that we can see. With radio telescopes, astronomers have very recently located the tiny central core that was left after the star blew up.

Radio telescopes in Australia. The round, white "dishes" detect radio waves from stellar explosions and other occurrences in outer space.

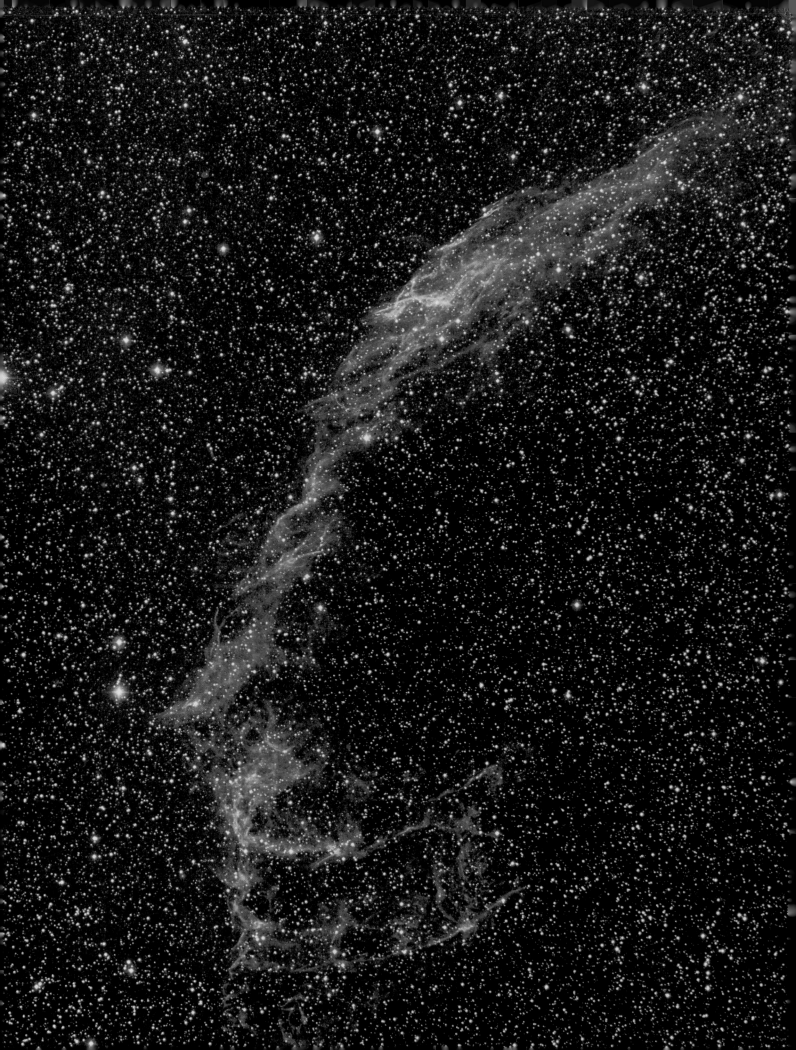

Another famous supernova remnant is the Veil Nebula in the constellation Cygnus. It is very faint and its striking beauty can be revealed only in photographs that require many minutes or hours to take. Much older than the Crab Nebula, it is estimated to have started from a supernova explosion some thirty to forty thousand years ago. The hot gases from the original star are still expanding outward into space.

The Veil Nebula in the constellation Cygnus is an ancient supernova remnant.

Cassiopeia A, a supernova remnant from a star that exploded about three hundred years ago.

Astronomers know of many other supernova remnants. Most, like the Veil Nebula, are so old that no one was around to record their beginnings. The largest one that is known is called the Gum Nebula, in honor of an astronomer who studied it extensively. The Gum Nebula covers almost a third of the sky, but the particles in it are so thinly spread out that it cannot be photographed. It can be detected only with special equipment. The Gum Nebula is estimated to have started expanding about twelve thousand years ago. It is the nearest supernova remnant known to us, and must have been created by the brightest supernova ever seen.

With the passage of time, all of the hot gases from aging stars cool off and float away, mingling with the particles of matter that are already present between the stars. This is the same material that eventually clumps into the kind of nebula where new stars are born. Our sun and solar system were formed from such particles—some from the original matter of the universe, and some from the gases that aging stars threw off during the last stages of their lives. The nebula that formed from all these particles no longer exists.

The earth from space. Can you detect the outline of South America beneath the swirling white clouds?

45

However, our planet, the earth, as well as everything we see around us, developed from that ancient nebula. Our houses, our food, our machines, and even our bodies are partially made from the material of stars that exploded and died long, long ago. So next time you look in the mirror, you might say hello to a star that lived billions of years before you were born.

The Milky Way Galaxy contains our solar system. It looks like the Andromeda Galaxy, pictured here. Our solar system formed from an ancient nebula in the Milky Way Galaxy.

Index

Italics indicate photographs.

For Further Reading

Consult any of the following sources for more in-depth information about nebulae.

Asimov, Isaac. *The Exploding Suns: The Secrets of Supernovas.* New York: E.P. Dutton, 1985.

Branley, Franklyn M. *Black Holes, White Dwarfs, and Super Stars.* New York: T. Y. Crowell, 1976.

Cooke, Donald A. *The Life and Death of Stars.* New York: Crown Publishers, 1985.

Fisher, David E. *The Creation of Atoms and Stars.* New York: H. H. Rineholt & Wilson, 1979.

Henbest, Nigel, and Marten, Michael. *The New Astronomy.* Cambridge: Cambridge University Press, 1983.

Jastrow, Robert. *Red Giants and White Dwarfs.* New York: W. W. Norton, 1979.

Odyssey, a children's astronomy magazine. Milwaukee: AstroMedia.

Any introductory astronomy textbook. Look up *Stellar evolution.*